Shekhinah Glory Exposed!

Shekhinah Glory Exposed!

The goddess not the glory

V. Lynn

Revelations Publishing House LLC

CONTENTS

CONTENTS

Conclusion

Shekhinah Glory Exposed!
The goddess not the glory

Mystery Babylon Series
www.revelationsbooks.com

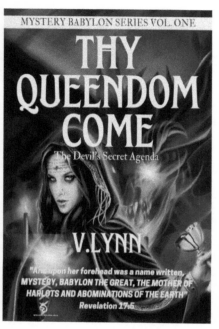

"An incredibly well researched book. This is information every person who loves and belongs Christ should read."

"This book gives a break down who "they" are, what "they" believe, why "they" hate you are why you are in their cross-hairs

"Brilliant Read! Very informativ this is that book you can't put down!"

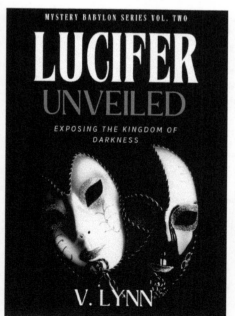

Introduction

Brothers and sisters: we are beyond a state of emergency. We are at the precipice of the prophecies of the end times being fulfilled. If you have not heard, the Euphrates River is drying up as it was prophesied in the book of Revelation. Every single unthinkable, unholy, unnatural, sacrilegious, blasphemous, and heretical sin listed in the Bible is acceptable in our current world. Everything the Lord hates and calls an abomination has been carefully woven into the fabric of not only society, but of Christendom. Throughout the millennia, centuries, and decades until the current time, societal norms have reversed; good is evil and evil is good. Men are women and women are men. The United States, specifically, has become the fulfillment of satanist *Aleister Crowley's*, "Do as thou Wilt" Law of Thelema, in all its Luciferian glory.

In the first volume of the Mystery Babylon Series, *Thy Queendom Come: The Devil's Secret Agenda*, an encapsulation of the agenda of Mystery Babylon is detailed. Mystery Babylon in the book included: the occult, secret societies, new age beliefs and practices, and religion of the *serpent's seed*. These practices and hidden ideologies have completely taken over the world. It is highly recommended that you read the entirety of *Thy Queendom Come* to fully grasp the blasphemy which we will speak of in this exposition.

To understand fully the gravity of today's agenda, you must comprehend the root of it. Whether those involved are aware of the root of this agenda or not, there is a reason for the aggressive totalitarian belief system being forced on society. It is being forced on us by politicians - on both sides of the aisle - and neither side is stopping or slowing down this agenda. Mainstream media, education, popular culture, entertainment, and unfortunately, some pulpits as well, are forcefully advancing the kingdom of darkness by ascribing to the tenets of this agenda, as well as participating in it. This campaign is moving at breakneck speed to bring in the New Order of the Ages, *Novus Ordo Seclorum*, as seen on the back of the U.S. dollar bill. The New World Order, which is also called the Aeon of Horus, the Golden Age, the Age of Aquarius, the coming Kingdom of Man, the New Atlantis etc., alongside the goal of every secret society and occult faction, from the garden until now, is the complete reversed transformation of God's original creation of man and woman, and everything else He created.

This agenda in plain face would never be accepted. No church or well-meaning social group, educational system, political party, or media forum would knowingly embrace such a demonic, satanic plot. Therefore, through social movements, such as feminism and the raising of the feminine over the masculine, we have reached a critical and dangerous mindset in that many woman believe men are not necessary. Role reversals have become prevalent and applauded. Sadly, many welcome this role reversal and view it as progression in human evolution. They are completely unaware that they are partaking in a satanic ritual to eradicate every system and the order our Creator put into place for mankind. *Do as Though Wilt* cannot achieve any more success than a person denying the very nature in which God created them.

This "gender" agenda is not a secular one, as many have been falsely led to believe. It is a religious and spiritual one orchestrated by the serpent's seed, to destroy "the seed of the woman." This agenda has been very clear for the last few decades. If it's not *Ariana Grande* singing "God is a Woman," it's a new movie called *The Woman King*, which was followed by the *Black Panther* sequel, which featured a female heroine in the role as the leader. A new series *Little Demon*, even gets in on the feminist action, depicting a 13-year-old girl as the antichrist - a figure typically portrayed as male. This little demon's mother is a powerful Wiccan, displaying countless body tattoos with a muscular frame and more masculine energy than *Denzel Washington* in *Training Day*. The devil himself in the series, portrayed by *Danny DeVito*, even utters the line, "the future is female."

These shows along with other societal churning, are actually the return of goddess worship, the Babylonian system, and temple prostitution. The United States is the home of the goddess. We have the biggest goddess sitting in the New York Harbor, the goddess of Liberty. The enemy slyly pulls on the heart strings of women everywhere, influencing them to embrace the tearing down of the *patriarchal system*. What we fail to understand is to tear down patriarchy on earth means to tear it down in heaven. To reverse the roles of women on earth, in the occult, means this is also happening in heaven - above. *As above, so below* is the Hermetic mantra of the occult.

Behind the veil of all the goddess worship, girl power, worship of the *divine feminine*, mother earth, sexual liberation of women, free spirits, independence, explosion of witchcraft and the occult, hides one of the MYSTERIES of Mystery Babylon - a name that is known to many as the Spirit of God, the Holy Spirit, the presence and the glory. This new term for Christendom, which crept into worship services, music, and even the names of several "church buildings," is the *Shekhinah*.

With no Biblical references to justify the use of this name, the church, trusted that this "oral tradition" represented the very Spirit, glory, and presence of God. Like Eve in the garden, unsuspecting believers blindly began using the term, *Shekhinah Glory*, and in a sense, treasured this name. Shekhinah Glory, as used in mainstream Christianity, only became popular less than a few decades ago. But, factually, it is thousands of years old.

As in any mystery, there are many layers to Shekhinah, ranging from the plausible and sensible, fanciful and whimsical to the absurd, obscene, idolatrous and UNFORGIVABLE. There is one sin in the Bible that is unforgivable, and that is, the BLASPHEMY AGAINST THE HOLY SPIRIT. Our Messiah himself, Jesus Christ, uttered these words in Matthew 12:31-32;

31 Wherefore I say unto you, All manner of sin and blasphemy shall be forgiven unto men: but the blasphemy against the Holy Ghost shall not be forgiven unto men. 32 And whosoever speaketh a word against the Son of man, it shall be forgiven him: but whosoever speaketh against the Holy Ghost, it shall not be forgiven him, neither in this world, neither in the world to come.

How does the Shekhinah mesh with the feminine uprising of today? The parallels will be shocking. As the layers peel from the veil of secrecy of the Shekhinah, "she", yes, "she" is not nearly the presence, Spirit or glory of God, as many have been told, but a separate, independent deity with a mind and opinion of her own – an opinion that is often *in opposition to the Father.*

"Now the serpent was more SUBTLE than any beast of the field." [Genesis 3:1].

There is no doubt, the serpent's seed slipped this word into worship services to move the children of the Most High to blaspheme against the Holy Spirit. And so be warned: once you come into the knowledge of the truth of Shekhinah, an immediate repentance and denouncement must take place. For those who refuse to see the truth and remain in error and gross blasphemy against the Holy Spirit by the synonymous use of this name and what it represents, I cannot make the judgement. Christ already has.

This short exposition is in compliment to *Thy Queendom Come*. The Shekhinah was a principal reason for the title of the book. Urgently, this companion book has been released. The church must be aware, of what and who it is they are calling on when they utter the phrase *Shekhinah Glory* and the origins from which it derives.

> "*For nothing is secret, that shall not be made manifest; neither anything hid, that shall*
> *not be known and come abroad.*" [Luke 8:17]

1

Talmud

Shekhinah is first mentioned in the Babylonian Talmud, literally, one of the most wicked, hateful, vile books in history. Many people are unaware, that after the crucifixion and resurrection of Jesus, those that were holding to their *own beliefs*, rejected traditional teachings. Christ was the fulfillment of the Old Testament prophecies, so in rejecting Christ, this sect, in essence, rejected the validity and authority of the Torah and the Old Testament. This is a fact not known to the average believer.

"The Babylonian Talmud is the culmination of the oral teachings of the scribes and Pharisees that Christ so adamantly rebuked. It is a long collection of books that weren't put into written form until around the 6th century A.D. It is composed of the Mishnah and Gemara, the rambling of Rabbis over the ages."

"Since the time of Moses, the modern-day people today known as Talmudists, have always attested their teachings were vocal, not written, chanted, not read, and *spell*-ed out, or recited. It's Hex instead of Text. Moses's laws to God were burned into stone, while the Talmudists claim they heard something. In it's whole, the Talmud is **the antithesis of Christianity**; It has nothing to do with the Old Testament." (Babylon's Most Unholy Book-AntiChrist Talmud, Sin to Win)

"The Talmud asserts Rabbis are superior to the biblical prophets and that the Jews must obey them even to the absurd point of abrogating Mosaic Law. As a result [they] prevented their children from studying the Bible, by placing the Talmud at the center of their educational curriculum." (Hoffman Rome Discovers the Talmud. Page 122)

"The Talmud is the lifeblood of the people. Most Judaism practiced today is not the Five Books of Moses. You would find it in the Talmud." -Rabbi Michael Stern

"Judaism is Talmudism, not Old Testament, and those who revere the Old Testament teachings outside the prism of Talmud are its hereditary enemies." (Hoffman, Judaism Discovered Page 205)

"But what of the Torah scrolls carried through the synagogues with such extreme reverence? Well, what of them? Every idolater reverences his totem-pole, but the worship of a dead thing does not give it life. The mutilated "sefer Torah" scrolls carried in the pagan synagogue rites, contain no vowels. The scrolls are composed entirely in consonants. These scrolls are almost unreadable and virtually meaningless." (Hoffman, Judaism Discovered Dead Ritual Fetish, The Torah Scrolls. Page 223)

"Judaism is not the religion of the Old Testament. Judaism is the religion of the Pharisees and is based on the Babylonian Talmud... And... remains by far the greatest danger in the world today, bar none." -Wolfgang Vollmar

"The message Satan has been whispering in the ears of those imbued with the unclean Talmudic/Kabbalistic spirit...is that the written text of the Old Testament is not sufficient. It is incomplete and lacking...Judaism teaches it is utterly incomprehensible and ultimately mute unless it is taught out of the mouths of Talmudic Rabbis." (Hoffman, Judaism Discovered Dead Ritual Fetish, The Torah Scrolls. Page 224)

Historian *Lloyd P. Gartner* of Tel-Aviv University concurs in his *History of the Jews in Modern Times*:
"Almost all Jews lived within the rich but constricted world of Judaism...Like Islam and Christianity, Judaism claims to be the truth...The path of life for a Jew was set forth in the sacred writings and summed up by Rabbinic sages in law codes, whose prime source was the Talmud and its interpreters." -*Isaac D'Israeli,* whose son *Benjamin D'Israeli* became British Prime Minister, declared, "The Talmud...forms a complete

system of the learning, ceremonies, civil and canon law of the Jews treating indeed on all subjects."

"In occult Judaism, the Talmud represents the bureaucratic right-hand path and the Kabbalah the mystical left-hand path, corresponding to male/female god-and goddess archetypes..." (Hoffman, Judaism Discovered Page 283)

Talmudic excerpts

- BT Shebuoth 9a; The old Testament's new moon goat sacrifice is to atone **for the sin of God.**

- BT Yebamoth 63a; Adam had sexual relations with all the animals in the Garden of Eden.

- BT Sanhedrin 66a; The commandment of Moses forbidding enchantments refers only to enchantments performed with weasels, birds or fish.

- BT Sanhedrin 76b, 78a; A man is not guilty of murder if he causes a poisonous snake to kill a man, the snake should be executed for murder, while the man goes free.

- BT Sanhedrin 78a; Killing a terminally ill person is not murder.

- BT Niddah 45a; Women cannot conceive before they reach twelve years and a day, according to the Rabbis. When asked how it was possible that a gentile girl had conceived at age six, the Rabbi replied **that gentiles are not human.**

- BT Sanhedrin 58b; A gentile who strikes a Jew deserves death, Striking a Jew is in God's eyes an assault on the Divine Presence.

- BT Sanhedrin 57a; A Jew need not pay a gentile the wages owed him for work.

- BT Baba Kamma 37b; The deeds of Israel are righteous, but the gentiles are capable only of sin.

- Hagigah 27a; declares no Rabbi can ever go to hell.

- BT Erubin 21b; Whosoever disobeys the Rabbis deserves death and will be punished by being boiled in hot excrement in hell.

- BT Baba Mezia 59b; A sly Rabbi debates God and through trickery defeats Him. **God admits the Rabbi won the debate.**

- BT Sanhedrin; A gentile who observes a day of rest deserves death.

- BT Abodah Zarah 22a; Gentiles are inclined to bestiality, lewdness and murder. Gentiles prefer sexual relations with cows more than their own wives. Eve had sexual intercourse with the serpent, transmitting lust to the gentiles from which Israelites are exempt.

- BT Sanhedrin 104a; God is displeased when Jews show hospitality to gentiles.

- BT Hagigah 13a; It is forbidden to teach gentiles the Law.

- BT Sanhedrin 59a; A gentile who studies the Law deserves death.

- BT Baba Kamma 113a; It is permissible to cheat a gentile in court.

- BT Baba Kamma 37b; The gentiles are outside the protection of the law and God has "exposed" their money to Israel.

- BT Sanhedrin 52b; A non-Jew is not considered a neighbor.

- BT Sanhedrin 57a; If a gentile kills a Jew, the gentile is to be killed. But if a Jew kills a gentile, **the Jew is to go free.**

- Yebamoth 98a; **All gentile children are animals.**

- Abodah Zarah 36b; **Gentile girls are in a state of niddah (filth) from birth.**

- BT Baba Bathra 16b; The birth of a girl is a sad occurrence.

- BT Sanhedrin 110b; Women are a vain treasure to their fathers.

- BT Yebamoth 59b; A woman who had intercourse with a beast is eligible to marry a Jewish priest. A woman who has sex with a demon is also eligible to marry a Jewish priest.

- BT Aboth; It is not good to talk to women, not even your own wife.

- BT Kiddushin 29b; It is forbidden to teach the Law to a woman.

- BT Gittin 91a; It is permissible to divorce your wife if she burns your dinner, or if you see a prettier girl.

- BT Avodah Zarah 17a; Christians are allied with hell, and Christianity is worse than incest. Going to prostitutes is the same as becoming a Christian.

- BT Rosh Hahanah 17a; Those who read the New Testament will have no portion in the world to come.

- BT Shabbat 116a; Jews must destroy the books of the Christians i.e. New Testament "The Books of the Minim" may not be save from a fire, but they must be burnt in their place.

- Sanhedrin 90a; Christians (min or minim) and others

who reject the Talmud will go to hell and be punished for all generations.

- Sanhedrin 59a; Murdering Goyim is like killing a wild animal.

- Libbre David 37; "To communicate anything to a Goy about our religious relations would be equal to the killing of all Jews., **for if the Goyim knew what we teach about them, they would kill us openly."**

"The murder of Christian missionaries is encouraged; "A person who proselytes any single Jew, whether man or woman, on behalf of false deities, should be stoned to death. This applies even if neither the proselyte or the Jew actually worshiped a false deity. As long as he instructed him to worship the false deity he should be executed by stoning." *Moses Maimonides*, Mishneh Torah, Hilchot Avodat Kochavim V'Chukkoteihem, 5:1

Yebamoth 55b; Intercourse is permitted with a dead relative regardless of whether she was single or married.

Ketuvot 11b; Rav Yehudah said in the name of Rav: A male child who has relations with a female adult causes her to be like one who was injured with a stick... Rava said: This is what was meant - an adult male who has relations with a female child has not done anything **because less than this [three years old] is like sticking a finger into an eyeball.**

Gitten 57A; Jesus is in hell. His punishment is being **boiled in hot semen**.

As distributing as that was to read, please keep in mind, this is the un-holy book, where the Shekhinah is derived.

2

Kabbalah

"In a word, Kabbalah or Qabalah or Cabala, IS THE MYSTERY RELIGION OF BABYLON. It's at the very core and essence of the mysteries, all new age teachings, witchcraft, Masonry and secret societies. All of the fundamental belief systems that shape what we know as the "mysteries," in theory, share the same root belief. Although various texts take on different forms, characters, gods, creation myths, and vary in concepts, theoretically, they all have the same end goal. Masters of the Kabbalah are considered the very highest in the mystery system. Kabbalah is extremely complex, and lately, it's been in public view, and there are versions, copies and guides. If you have dabbled in Tarot cards, Gematria, gnomes, reincarnation, angel numbers, metaphysics, magic, used the term "left" or "right," used talking points like "the universe," "vibe," "higher conscious," ascribe to "gender bending" theology, it all can be traced back to the Babylonian Talmud and hence, the Kabbalah, and, that is only the very brief beginnings." (Lynn Chapter 33 Mystery Book)

"Kabbalah" is the unacknowledged religion of the West, a fact that will become evident over time. It is the belief system of Freemasonry and organized Jewry, the two forces that govern the world. It is the reason God and the Ten Commandments have been banished from public life, why Christianity has been gutted and replaced by moral "relativity." (Evans, Richard)

"In the eyes of the Kabbalist the Zohar assumed an importance greater even than that of the Talmud. It's dicta were held in greater veneration than those of rabbinical literature. In comparing them with the rationalists, that is, the Talmudist, the Zohar classifieds the Mystics as clairvoyance or seers, those who probe beneath the surface." (Bension The Spanish Mystics. Page 22)

Note: The Zohar is the holiest book of the Kabbalah.

"Cabala this was amongst the ancient Jews a mystical philosophy, in as much as they professed to possess cabalistic secrets from the earliest ages, even from the days of Adam." (Macoy Page 445-446)

"In order to understand what's going on in the world and within Christianity we need to have at least a basic understanding of Kabbalah, as it is the foundation of all false religion. ... Kabbalah's Oneism is at the core of science and how it has seeped into all denominations." (Nachtigal)

"The Kabbalah, literally 'tradition,' that is, the tradition of things divine, is the sum of Jewish mysticism. It has had a long history and for centuries has exerted a profound influence on those among the Jewish people who were eager to gain a deeper understanding of the traditional forms and conceptions of Judaism." (Scholem, The Kabbalah and It's Symbolism Introduction. Page 1)

"This Kabbalistic world of the sefirot encompasses what philosophers and theologians called the world of the divine attributes. But to the mystics it was divine life itself, insofar as it moves toward Creation. The hidden dynamic of this life fascinated the Kabbalists, who found it reflected in every realm of Creation. But this life as such is not separate from, or subordinate to, the Godhead, rather, it is the revelation of the hidden root, concerning which, since it is never manifested, not even in symbols, nothing can be said, and which the Kabbalists called Ein Sof, the infinite. But this hidden root and the divine emanations are one." (Scholem, The Kabbalah and It's Symbolism Chapter 2 The Meaning of the Torah. Page 35-36)

"The conception of God's name as the highest concentration of divine power forms a connecting link between two sets of ideas, the one originally associated with magic, the other pertaining to mystical speculation as such. The idea of the magic structure and nature of the Torah may be found long before the Kabbalah, in a relatively early midrash, for example, where in commenting on Job 38:13; 'No man knoweth its order,' Rabbi Eleazar declares: 'The various sections of the Torah were not given in their correct order. For if they had been given in their correct order, anyone who read them would be able to wake the dead and perform miracles." (Scholem Chapter 2 The Meaning of the Torah. Page 37)

"Men could now use that same language in **speaking to the angels who ran the universe and create wonders by their very words.**" (Hoffman Reuchlin v Pfefferkorn. Page 232)

"The key linking heaven and earth is the **Hebrew names of the angels.** Since the angels move the heavenly bodies, they can be ordered or beseeched to create wonders on earth. Magic is the word of God, but not in the sense that the Gospel is the word of God." (Hoffman Reuchlin v Pfefferkorn. Page 251)

"In Cabala, evil takes on a mysterious existence of its own, which its precepts trace back to the physical appearance of life on earth, or Adam. Cabala claims that Adam throws the entire stream of life out of balance, and that the Church, or Christianity, by formalizing the physical **existence of the Adamite people on earth, have become a problem which must be resolved.** This is the essence of the basic anti-life principle underlying all Cabala and its heir, Freemasonry. These precepts declare that Satanism will achieve its final triumph over the Church and Christianity, thus ending the "dualism" of this world, the struggle between good and evil. In short, the problem of good and evil will be ended when evil triumphs and good is eliminated from the earth. This program may sound somewhat simplistic, but it is the basic premise of the Cabala and Freemasonry." (The Serapeum)

Ein Sof

Septinorum Tree
from *Portae Lucis* by Paulus Ricius (Augsburg, 1516)

Ein Sof

"In the Kabbalah it is taught that the highest and most
mysterious God or Power or whatever else we may choose
to call it, Ein Sof, Pure thought, Supreme will, this was not
composed of matter it was purely spiritual. From Ein Sof
there were ten emanations of spiritual beings. The Kabbalah
stated that the Holy Ghost made all things male or female,
because otherwise nothing could endure. It described the
archetypal man using many mystic references of Gematria, to

the particular numerical values of words, and to the sex of the left and the right side."

- Wisdom was located in the forehead and was male

- Intelligence was located in the left side of the chest and was female

- Wisdom the father, and intelligence, the mother produced a CROWN

- Love was male and was in the right arm

- Justice was female and resided in the left arm, together they produce beauty, residing in the bosom or breast.

- Firmness was male and resided in the right thigh and splendor was female and resided in the left thigh, together they produce foundation or sex or sexual organs. (Gramassi)

Ten Divine Powers (Sefirot)

There are ten divine powers of the Ein Sof known as the ten *Sefirot*. The second is the identification of one of the ten divine powers, separate from the nine, *as feminine.* Thus begins the **gender dualism** into the divine realms.

"The author of the *Tikhmim* identifies the *Shekhinah*, God's presence, conceived as the last of the ten emanations, or

Sefirot, with the Torah in its total manifestations, embracing all its meanings and levels of meaning. Accordingly, we also call it nut, and King Solomon said when he entered this Paradise [of mystical speculation]: "I went down into the garden of nuts" (Song of Songs 6: I I). (Scholem, The Kabbalah and It's Symbolism In Jewish Mysticism. Page 58-59)

"The word Shekhinah is not found in the Bible. It was formulated in [Babylonian] Talmudic literature from the verb designating the residence Shekhinah of God in the temple in Jerusalem among the Jewish people. Shekhinah is used in rabbinic literature as one of the many abstract titles or references of God, like "The Holy Blessed One Be He"... Other theories in the development of the Shekhinah is that it was not originally describe as feminine and **also it was an angel."** (Dan Page 45-52)

This diagram (above), which may be familiar to you, is in essence, the BODY OF GOD, this is God uncovered, this is how the Kabbalists claim that the, UNIVERSE of God is divided up. The Kabbalist have *attempted* to, "Uncover the nakedness of the Father, as Pastor Chuck Misler described in his sermon on the Kabbalah. (Misler)

The very last "emanation" or sefirot, the one on the bottom, is the only "female" emanation, who is in fact, the *Shekinah,* or as many refer to, the 10th sefirot.

For every noun in the Hebrew language has either a

masculine or feminine gender except a few. The two Biblical names of God, Yahweh (pronounced, out of reverence for its great holiness, as "Adonai" and usually translated as "the Lord" and Elohim (or briefly El; translated as "God") are masculine. When a pronoun is used to refer to God, it is the masculine "He", when a verb describes that He did something or an adjective qualifies Him, they appear in the masculine form." (Patai Introduction. 3 The Masculine Godhead. Page 21)

Shekhinah

"The term is extremely common in Talmudic literature from about the first century BCE or the first center CE but does not appear in either the Bible or in non-rabbinic writings, despite some abortive efforts to discover it, disguised, in translations, especially in the New Testament (as in the first Chapter of John)."(Scholem, On the Mystical Shape of the

Godhead; Basic concepts in Kabbalah Shekhinah the Feminine Element in Divinity. Page 147)

"Shekhinah first appeared in the Aramaic translation-paraphrase of the Bible called *Targum Onkelos*, scholars debate this works origin anywhere from first century to the fourth century A.D. Shekhinah (sh'khinah) is a Hebrew abstract noun derived from the Biblical verb *shakhan* and meaning literally "the act of dwelling." The abstract nouns, constructed from the verbal root-letters with the added -ah suffix, make the word of a feminine gender. This work the Targum Onkelos, whenever the manifestation of God's presence was mentioned or perceived used the term Shekhinah. For example the verse Let them make Me a Sanctuary that I may dwell (w'shakhanti) among them, is rendered "Let them make before Me a Sanctuary that I may let My Shekhinah dwell among them. The Targum, evidently could not tolerate a direct reference to God even in a poetic text, as it paraphrases "He (God) found him (Israel) in a desert land...He compassed him about...as, "He filled their needs in a desert land...He let them dwell around His Shekhinah." (Patai Chapter 4. The Shekhina. Pag 140-141)

"This presentation of the Shekhinah as female element -simultaneously **mother, bride and daughter-within the structure of the Godhead** constitutes a very meaningful step, with far-reaching consequences, one which the Kabbalists attempted to justify by Gnostic interpretation." (Scholem, On the Mystical Shape of the Godhead; Basic concepts in Kabbalah Shekhinah the Feminine Element in Divinity. Page 160)

"During the thirteenth century, when Kabbalism invested Judaism with a new vitality, she [goddess] emerged as a distinct female deity, **possessing a will and desire of her own, acting independently of the traditional but somewhat shrunken masculine God, often confronting and occasionally opposing Him, and playing a greater role than He in the affairs of Her children,** the people of Israel...although often still called by her old name Shekhinah, assumed another name as well, more fitting to her new and high status, Matronit, the Matron, Lady or Queen." (Patai Introduction. 5. The Hebrew Goddess. Page 26-27)

"Shekhinah is the frequently used TALMUDIC term denoting the visible and audible manifestation of God's presence on earth. In it's ultimate development as it appears in the late Midrash literature, the Shekhinah concept stood for **an independent, feminine divine entity** prompted by her compassionate nature to argue with God in defense of man. She is thus, if not by character, then by function and position a direct heir to such ancient Hebrew goddesses of Canaanite origin as **Asherah and Anath.**" (Patai Chapter 4. The Shekhina. Page 137)

"In the development of the Talmudic Shekhinah, God's attributes or as the common Gnostic term "emanations" developed from the character of God to actual entities or angelic like beings. One such attribute was Wisdom in which Solomon in Proverbs, and Job referred to Wisdom as "she." Philosopher *Philo* (c. 20 BCE – c. 50 CE, a Hellenistic Jewish philosopher who lived in Alexandria, in the Roman province of Egypt) (Philo) states, "unequivocally that God is the husband of Wisdom."

"Wisdom (Hokhma) played a particularly important role among Jewish Gnostics. The myth is as follows:

"Out of the primeval chaos, God created the seven archons through the intermediacy of his Wisdom, which was identical with the "dew of light." Wisdom now cast her eidolon, or shadow-image upon the primeval waters of the Tohu wa-Bohu, whereupon the archons formed the world and the body of man. Man crawled about the earth like a worm, until Wisdom endowed him with spirit. Satan, in the shape of a serpent, had intercourse with Eve who thereupon bore Cain and Abel. Thus sexuality became the original sin." (Patai Chapter 4. The Shekhinah. Page 139).

"Wisdom was then seen bringing the flood to earth, sent seven prophets from Moses to Ezra (corresponding to the seven planets). In this myth Wisdom, acting like a female deity, clearly resembles the Gnostic concept of the anima mundi, the "world-soul." (Patai Chapter 4. The Shekhinah. Page 139-140)

Shekhinah Speaks

A Talmudic passage describe it as "the Shekhinah rang before him (Samson) like a bell.

"According to a Palestinian view, transmitted to Babylonia by *Rab Dimi* (early 4th century A.D.), the Shekhinah spoke to Adam, to the Serpent, and to the fishes, and, as a consequence of this distinction, members of these three species copulate face to face position, while all other animals perform the sexual act fact to back." (Patai Chapter 4. The Shekhinah. Page 145-146)

"*A.A Marmorstein* has convincingly show, these two concepts were used synonymously in the Talmudic period, When, therefore a Talmudic teacher speaks of the Holy Spirit, he may as well have used the term Shekhinah." (Patai Chapter 4. The Shekhinah. Page 148)

"*Rabbi Aha* (circa 300 A.D.) said "The Holy Spirit comes to the defense (of sinful Israel by) saying first to Israel; "Be not a witness against thy neighbor without a cause, and thereafter saying to God; "Say not; I will do to him as he hath done to me." We have here a very early testimony as to the idea that the "Holy One, blessed by He" or God, and the Shekhinah or Holy Spirit, are two separate and discrete divine entities...She was therefore considered to have an opinion, a mind, a will and a personality of her own. She is opposed to God and tries to influence him." (Patai Chapter 4. The Shekhina. Pag 148-149)

"Through this identification, everything that is said in the Talmudic interpretations of the Song of Songs about the Community of Israel as daughter and bride was transferred to the Shekhinah. It is impossible, I believe, to say which was the primary factor: the revival by the earliest Kabbalists of the idea of a feminine element in God, or the exegetic identification of the previously distinct concepts of the Ecclesia and the Shekhinah, the specifically Jewish metamorphosis in which so much of the Gnostic substance entered into Jewish tradition." (Scholem Chapter 3 Kabbalah and Myth. Page 106)

"But here it must be stressed that these almost demonic aspects of the Shekhinah as 'lower mother' do not yet appear in the 'upper mother,' the third sefirah, which, to be sure, is a *demiurge* (yotser bereshith), but in a positive sense, free from the pejorative shading attaching to the term in the old Gnostic systems. Strange and contradictory motifs are woven into a unique whole in this symbolism of the third sefirah, which as primordial mother of all being is particularly 'charged' with myth."

"In every exile into which the children of Israel went, the Shekhinah was with them.'1 In the Talmud this means only that God's presence was always with Israel in its exiles. In the Kabbalah, however, it is taken to me and that a part of **God Himself is exiled from God**. These two ideas, the exile of the Ecclesia of Israel in the Midrash and the exile of the soul from its original home-a conception found in many religions and not only among Gnostics-fused in the Kabbalist myth of the exile of the Shekhinah." (Scholem Chapter 3 Kabbalah and Myth. Page 107)

Power

Shekhinah's Power

"Expressed in a *Tannaitic* passage which states on ten occasions did the Shekhinah descend from on High,

- After the fall, when she entered the Garden of Eden to punish Adam, Eve and the Serpent

- She confused the builders at the Tower of Babel

- She destroyed Sodom and Gomorrah

- She saved the Children of Israel from Egyptian Slavery

- She drowned the Egyptians in the Sea of Reeds

- She appeared on Mt. Sinai

- She led the Children of Israel in the pillar of cloud

- She entered the Sanctuary

- Will once more appear in the future battle of *Gog and Magog*

Goddess

Astarte statue

"The Shekhinah is not God and she is not of God. She is not the Biblical woman who shall crush the head of the serpent. She is an idol, the manifestation of the thousand faces of the strange gods: *Lilith*, *Astarte*, the Canaanite goddess *Qadesh*, *Demeter* and *Isis*. Shekhinah/Lilith is the sorceress who wields the sacred name of Yahweh..."

Astarte

"*Anath, Lady of Heaven*, mistress of all gods. *Astarte* the consort of Chemosh, Moab's national god. Later period Astarte becomes the chief goddess of the Sidonians replacing Asherah. The Kings of Sidon were also priest of Astarte and their wives had the title of "priestess of Astarte." Sidonian King Eshmun'azar and his mother built a temple for Astarte at Sidon-by-the-Sea. The city of Ashtartu in the Bashan is referred to several times in the Bible as a city of Levites. Once it is called Be'eshterah, once "Ashterah," but usually Ashtaroth, in the plural form. Ashtaroth was originally the capital city of Og, the legendary giant king of Bashan, and of his people the Rephaim who were smitten by *Chedorlaomer.* This semi historical, semi-mythical record references the full name of the city as Ashteroth-Qarnaim i.e Astarte of the Two Horns. The original meaning of the name Astarte was **"that which issues from the womb."**

Astarte's proper name is *Anath*, such as Baal's proper name was *Hadd.*

"She is the daughter of *El*, the god of heaven and his wife *Lady Asherah of the Sea*. She has many features in common with Sumerian Inanna and the Akkadian Ishtar of Mesopotamia. Anath spent much time on the battlefield. She was a goddess of love, both chaste and promiscuous. She was epitomized in a 13th century Egyptian text in which her and Astarte are called "the goddesses who conceive but do not bear" meaning they are perennially fruitful without ever losing their virginity." Author *Phil Byblius* identifies Anath with Athena, the virgin goddess of the Greeks. Anath is also called "lady of heaven, mistress of all the gods." She also had lovers of gods, men and animals. Her foremost lover was her BROTHER Baal. When she approached Baal he dismissed his other wives. In preparation for her union with him she bathed in sky-dew and rubbed herself with ambergris from a sperm whale."

> Ambergis : a waxy substance found floating in or on the shores of tropical waters, believed to originate in the intestines of the sperm whale, and used in perfumery as a fixative (Merriam-Webster).

The intimate encounters with Baal and Anath are explicit and graphic even among near Eastern texts. "In a place called Dubr, Baal lay seventy-seven times with Anath who assumed the shape of a heifer for the occasion, and a wild bull was a result of this union. Anath had a mortal lover called Aqhat who Anath addressed as "My darling great big he-man."Anath was a wet nurse of the gods. And also regarded as the wife of the Egyptian god Seth. An Egyptian magical text from the 13th century describes in sadistic terms how Seth "deflowers" Anath on the seashore. No Near Eastern goddess was more blood thirsty than Anath. She was easily provoked to violence and once she began a battle, she would destroy anything in her path. She got pleasure out of fighting and would fight people in the East and West. Anath decapitated people and if that wasn't gruesome enough, it is said, "She binds their severed heads to her back and their cut off hands to her girdle, and plunges knee-deep in the blood of troops, and hip-deep in the gore of heroes." She protected the Pharoah in Egypt and in Egypt was known as, "the goddess, the victorious," **a woman acting as a man, clad as a male and girt as a female."**

"In Judaism, the esoteric teaching is that the Judaic male in general and the rabbinic sage in particular, together with the goddess Shekhinah are like unto God."

"Worship of the Shekhinah in the form of the *moon goddess* is a formal rite in Orthodox Judaism. Orthodox Judaism is s**teeped in moon worship and lunar associations.** In BT Sanhedrin 4 it is stated that "sanctifying the moon is akin to greeting the Shekhinah.""

"Maimonides proposes that the right intention for anybody who is praying-not only a blind person or someone who cannot tell the cardinal points-is to visualize himself as if standing in Heaven, before the Shekhinah." (Mock)

"Various forms of black magic, superstition, goddess-worship, reincarnation and idolatry incontrovertibly comprise the under-publicized, formative care of Judaism's oral traditions...since their sojourn in Babylon 1800 years ago." (Hoffman, Jewish Spirit Talmudist Kabbalism Discovered Redemption through Evil. Page 241)

Divine feminine

"G-d as She. The word Shekhinah is feminine, and so when we refer to G-d as the Shekhinah, we say "She." Of course, we're still referring to the same One G-d, just in a different modality.

"After all, you were probably wondering why we insist on calling G-d "He." We're not talking about a *being* limited by any form—certainly not a body that could be identified as male or female. But consider this: As soon as we just in that duality, we take the female role, so that He calls us She and we call Him He. Begin to refer to G-d, we have already compromised His oneness. Because we have already created a duality —there is us and there is G-d. Then we do whatever we can to mend the schism between us and return to one." (Freeman)

"Where can we find a powerful image of the Divine feminine within Jewish sources? One name for Her which has been with us for centuries is the Shekhinah, the "dweller within." (Hammer)

"We also cannot forget that the images and stories of the Shekhinah are connected to traditions of the Divine feminine around the world, from the ancient goddess Innanna, who is described as a warrior for her people just as the Shekhinah is in the Zohar; to the Virgin Mary, who is an intercessor in matters of Divine judgment like the Shekhinah; to Kuan Yin of Asia, who embodies compassion for those who suffer, just as the Shekhinah does. Jews have been afraid to acknowledge the Shekhinah's relationship to goddesses and goddess-like images because of the traditional Jewish prohibition against idolatry. Yet to deny our connection to the Divine feminine as it is expressed and loved by others is to deny our connection to the human, and feminine, religious experience, and to render invisible some of the sources of our own spirituality." ibid

"The Shekhinah allows us to break through the exclusively male and hierarchical visions of God and imagine a God that changes as we change, that evokes nature as well as the supernatural. *Melissa Weintraub* writes: "Shekhinah, Mother of all being, you are the stream that runs through our veins, and dances through the soil...." When we speak to the immanent Shekhinah, She speaks not to us, but through us, and through all the varied facets of the world." ibid

6

Lilith

Lilith

You may have seen or heard about *Lilith*, the Babylonian/
Sumerian demon who is most known for seducing men and
also being the mythical first wife of Adam. Lilith is bought to
you by the way of the Talmud, and yes, there is a connection
between Lilith and Shekhinah.

"The she-demons of yore, *Lilith, Naamah, Igrath bath*

Mahalath, who first appear in Talmudic literature as lowly and hairy female ghouls, and who managed to work themselves up to much higher position, until their queen, **Lilith, become God's consort**. This happened following the **destruction of the Jerusalem Temple** and the subsequent exile of Israel, which came to be regarded as catastrophic events not only for the people but also for God." (Patai Introduction. 5. The Hebrew Goddess. Page 27)

> *Luke 21:5 And as some spake of the temple, how it was adorned with goodly stones and gifts, he said,6 As for these things which ye behold, the days will come, in the which there shall not be left one stone upon another, that shall not be thrown down.*

"Lilith's epithet was "the beautiful maiden," but she was believed to have been a harlot and a vampire who, once she chose a lover would never let him go, without ever giving him real satisfaction. She was unable to have children and had no milk in her breasts." (Patai Chapter 7 Lilith. Page 208)

"In Babylonian terracotta reliefs, she is shown as slender, well-shaped, beautiful and nude with human eyes, wings and owl feet, she stands on two lions who are turned away from each other and flanked by owls. On her head she wore a cap with horns, in her hands she holds a ring and rod combination. This brings Lilith from a demon to a goddess who tames wild beasts and rules the night. In the seventh century B.C a tablet found at Arslan Tash in northern Syria shows her as a winged sphinx across whose body is written in Phoenician/ Canaanite dialect: "O, Flyer in a dark chamber, Go await at once, O Lili!" (Patai Chapter 7 Lilith. Page 208)

"Then there is Lilith, a mythic figure whom the tradition demonized but who for some is the embodiment of sexuality and freedom...." (Hammer)

Lilith and Samael

Satan in Jewish lore is known as *Samael*.

Lilith's births variations (according to Kabbalistic and Talmudic traditions);

"Created before Adam on the fifth day of creation, because the "living creature" with whose swarms God filled the waters was Lilith.

"Created in the same manner in which He had shortly

before fashioned Adam. For reasons unknown it is claimed that God used the earth (not Adam's body) filth and impure sediments from the earth to form the female, and thus this creature "female" was evil."

"A third version claims Lilith's soul was lodged in the depths of the Great Abyss whence she was called forth and was joined to Adam. When Adam was created and his body completed a thousand souls from the left (evil) side tried to attach themselves to him. But God let out a shout and drove them off. All this while Adam was green without a soul, then a cloud descended and God commanded the earth to produce a living soul, now Adam was able to stand up and his female was attached to his side. But God sawed his creature into two whereupon Lilith flew off to the cities of the Sea where she still lurks ready to harm mankind."

"Another version says Lilith was not created by God, but as a divine entity which emerged spontaneously either out of the Great Supernal Abyss or out of the power aspect of God (the Gevurah or Din) which manifests itself chiefly in the divine acts of stern judgement and punishment. This stern punitive aspect of God, one of his ten mystical attributes (Sephirot) has it's lowest manifestation some affinity with the realm of evil referred to as "the dregs of the wine," and it is out of this that Lilith emerged together with Samael."

"They (Samael and Lilith) are red like the rose, and they spread out into several sides and paths. The male is called

Samael, and his female (Lilith) is always contained in him. The female of Samael is called SERPENT, WOMAN OF HAR-LOTRY END OF ALL FLESH END OF DAYS." (Patai Chapter 7 Lilith. Page 218-219)

"In the mystical writings of *Jacob* and *Isaac Hacohen* of Segovia, Castile; Lilith and Samael are said to have been born **by emanation from beneath the Throne of Glory in the shape of an androgynous, double-faced being,** corresponding, in the spiritual realm to the birth of Adam and Eve who too were born as hermaphrodite. The two androgynous twin couples not only resembled each other, but both "were like the image of what is above" that is reproduced, in a visible form, the image of the androgynous deity." (Patai Chapter 7 Lilith. Page 219)

"According to Kabbalist *Naphtali Herz ben Jacob Elhanan* (mid 16th century), in the second of the seven earth layers, from the bottom abide the "giant human figures, tall of stature who were born of Adam in the 130 years during which he begot demons, spirits and Lilin. Lilith used to come to him against his will and conceive from Adam. And these beings are always sad and full of sorrow and sighs. These hosts can multiply and ascend to this world and become harmful spirits and then return to their abode." (Patai Chapter 7 Lilith. Page 221)

Lilith as Succuba

"She forsakes the husband of her youth, Samael, and descends to earth and fornicates with men who sleep here below in the uncleanness of emission. And from them are born demons, spirits and Lilin and they are called the "plagues of mankind.""

"Lilith is well capable of seducing men not only in their sleep but also while awake. Once she succeeds, she turns from a beautiful seductress into a cruel fury and kills her victim. She adorns herself with many ornaments like a despicable harlot and takes up her position at the crossroads to seduce the sons of man. When a fool approaches her, she grabs him, kisses him, and pours him wine of dregs of viper's gall. As soon as he drinks it, he goes astray after her. When she see's he has gone astray after her from the path of truth, she divests herself of all ornaments which she put on for that fool. Her ornaments for the seduction of the sons of man are;

Her hair is long and red like the rose
Her cheeks are white and red
From her ears hang six ornaments
Egyptian chords and ornaments from the East
Her mouth is set like a narrow door comely in décor
Her tongue is sharp like a sword, words smooth like oil
Lips are red like a rose and sweetened by the world
She is dressed in scarlet and adorned with forty ornaments less one.

"Yon fool goes astray after her and drinks from the cup

of his wife and commits with her fornications and strays after her."

"...She then flies to heaven, denounces him and when he thinks he can "have" her as before she removes her ornaments and turns into a menacing figure and stands before him clothed in garments of flaming fire, inspiring terror and making body and soul tremble, full of frightening eyes, in her hand a drawn sword dripping bitter drops. She then kills that fool and casts him into Gehenna." (Patai Chapter 7 Lilith. Page 222-223)

"Lilith tried to seduce Jacob but she was no match for him, he escaped and Samael attacked him but could not prevail."

"All the illegitimate children that a man has begotten with demons in the course of his life appear after his death to take part in the mourning for him and in his funeral. For all those spirits that have built their bodies from a drop of his seed regard him as their father. And so, especially on the day of his burial, he must suffer punishment; for while he is being carried to the grave, they swarm around him like bees, crying: 'You are our father,' and they complain and lament behind his bier, because they have lost their home and are now being tormented along with the other demons which hover [bodiless] in the air. According to others, the demons claim their inheritance on this occasion along with the other sons of the deceased and try to harm the legitimate children. Those who dance seven times round the dead man do so in order to form a sacral circle, which will prevent these unlawful children from approaching the deceased." (Scholem Page 155)

"They firmly believe that if a man's seed escapes him, it gives rise, with the help of *mahlath* [a female demon] and Lilith, to evil spirits, which however "die" when the time comes. When a man dies and his children begin to weep and lament, these *shedim*, or evil spirits, come too, wishing, along with the other children, to have their part in the deceased as their father; they tug and pluck at him, so that he feels the pain, and God himself, when He sees this noxious offspring by the corpse, is reminded of the dead man's sins. It is known to me that ...s in their lifetime sternly ordered their children not to make the slightest plaint or weep until the dead body in the cemetery had been purified by washing, cleansing, and the cutting of the finger- and toenails, because these unclean spirits are thought to have no further part in the body, once it is cleansed." (Scholem Page 156)

"The marriage between Samael and Lilith was arranged by the "Blind Dragon" who in Kabbalistic mythology is the counterpart on high of the "dragon that is in the sea." There is a dragon of the above who is the blind prince and he functions as the intermediary between Samael and Lilith and his name is Taniniver...on the left there is the shape of a serpent riding in a blind dragon, on this dragon rides on Lilith the wicked, may she be destroyed quickly in our days."

However, the marriage of Lilith with Samael also known as

the "Angel Satan" or the "Other God" was not allowed to prosper. **God castrated Samael.** This myth found in 17th century Kabalistic books, is based on the identification of "Leviathan the slant serpent and Leviathan the tortuous serpent" with Samael and Lilith respectively and on the reinterpretation of the old Talmudic myth according to which God castrated the male Leviathan and killed the female in order to prevent them from coupling and destroying the earth. Leviathan the serpent is, to the Kabbalists, Lilith who seduces men to follow crooked paths." (Patai Chapter 7 Lilith. Page 234-235)

Lilith and Shekhinah

"Treatise on the Emanations on the Left. This treatise (circa 1265) describe seven divine evil powers, the first of which is Samael and the seventh feminine one is Lilith, combined together by *Rabbi Isaac ben Jacob ha-Cohen* **as a divine couple parallel to Shekhinah.** The evil pair rule over a diverse structure of evil demons, who struggle for universal domination against the powers of goodness, the *Emanations on the Right.* The realm of evil includes images of snakes, dragons and monsters." (Dan Page 45-52)

- Both emanated as an emanation of the deity

- Both are "virgins"

- Both are promiscuous

- Both are queens, Shekhinah-Matronit the heavenly queen of Israel, Lilith the queen of Sheba and Ze-margad.

- Motherly; Matronit gives birth to innumerable souls, Matronit's souls are pure through husbands and wives, Lilith's are impure and are demons.

- Both are goddesses of war

- Wives, Matronit of Jacob and Moses, Lilith of Adam and Cain

- Both became the wife of *god*. Matronit during the dedication of the Temple, Lilith after it's destruction

- Both were enjoyed carnally by Samael

"Triangle, "God is one, but the goddess who is part of him is two, **the Matronit and Lilith**. She appears like the revolving flame of the Cherubim's sword in the ancient myth, once she shows her Matronit-face, once her Lilith visage."

"The bogus claim that Lilith and Shekhinah are two distinct entities representing separate forces of black magic and white magic is strictly for the *peti yaamin lekhol davar*."
(Hoffman, Judaism Discovered Page 268)

7

Tetragrammaton

**CREATION VI
TETRAGRAMMATON**

"Y-H-W-H is known as the Tetragrammaton to the Kabbalists and Talmudist."

"Aleister Crowley [famed satanist]has a Tetragrammaton for magick." (see below reference).

Aleister Crowley's Pentagram

"In researching this book [Thy Queendom Come], there were several times when many subjects seemed too dark to venture upon, review or study. The Tetragrammaton being one. I saw this name once and it was labeled "The secret name of YHWH," this chilled me to the bone. Why? Because behind their alpha- bet, codes, and all the secret society weavings and magic, I truly felt something was more sinister about this than others. The use of God's name for manipulating God's presence, bordered on, if not exceeded, apostasy. The Kabbalist whole operation is based upon the name of God. How had they come up with an advanced-sounding name like the Tetragrammaton for the sovereign God? Remember, this name is NOT in the BIBLE."

"Why would one of the most wicked men that ever lived, Aleister Crowley have a symbol with the supposed Holy Name of God in a pentagram? Why was Kabbalah not just found in every book of magic, it IS the very root of it, none excluded. So a book used for magic, has a secret name for

God? Furthermore, you cannot manipulate our Jehovah! He doesn't answer to manipulated versions of his name, nor can his presence be summoned. It was extremely difficult, but I found something, and it left me asking the question, who do these Talmudists and Kabbalists serve? One thing is for sure, they do not serve the God of the BIBLE." (Lynn Chapter 35 Serpent's Seed)

"Now, as to all that has been said, the intelligent Freemason will at once see its application to the third degree. Of all the degrees of Freemasonry, this is by far the most important and sublime. The solemn lessons which it teaches, the sacred scene which it represents, and the impressive ceremonies with which it is conducted, are all calculated to inspire the mind with feelings of awe and reverence."

"Into the holy of holies of the temple, when the ark of the covenant has been deposited in its appropriate place, and the **Shekhinah** was hovering over it, the high priest alone, and on one day only in the whole year, was permitted, after the most careful purification, to enter with bare feet, and to pronounce, with fearful veneration, the **Tetragrammaton** or omnific word. (Mackey Chapter 19 Rite of Discalceation. Page 128)

"According to the Zohar [Kabbalah], The supernal Mother "H" impregnated by the Father "Y," gave birth to "W" the son, whereupon she stood up and suckled him. And when the W emerged, his female male the Daughter (second "H") emerged together with him. In another version the son and daughter were thus born as a single but androgynous being."

These four divine concepts of the Tetragrammaton supposedly reveal the hidden name and nature of the godhead, which is not a "trinity" but in essence a family [father, mother, sister and brother) which form the Kabbalistic TETRAD or godhead.

Reference:

Aleister Crowley

Edward Alexander Crowley, who came to be more popularly known as Aleister Crowley, was a magician, occultist, painter, writer, active mountaineer and founder of the Thelema religion. Some people even believe that he was actually a member of the British intelligence agency and even Crowley had himself claimed that once. His mother named him the beast, he called himself 666. (The Famous People)

8

Tetrad

The four deities of *Tetrads* always make up some natural, cosmic or atmospheric element of earth and the heavens, such as; air, rain, vegetation, storm, heaven, sea, time, earth, sky, abundance etc. Also humanistic or daily life aspects such as love, marriage, childbirth, heath, abundance, light, darkness, wisdom and war.

"As concerning the goddess in several Tetrads, all have the aspect of love as well as war."

"In the ancient Canaanite pantheon itself the four gods El, Ashera, Baal and Anath stand among all the other gods as a clearly recognizable divine family."

"In Greek mythology, Cronus, Rhea, Zeus and Hera seem to have formed the original divine tetrad. Cronus and Rhea were brother and sister as well as husband and wife."

"Roman equivalent was Saturn, Ops, Jupiter and Juno Lucina or Lucetia, referring to her original light-nature. In her capacity as the goddess of marriage, she was also known as Matrona, a name which of course, reminds us of the Kabbalistic name of the daughter-goddess, the Matronit." (Patai Chapter 5 The Kabbalistic Tetrad. Page 167)

"In the Kabbalah the Tetragrammaton is given in sexual-familial terms. "The Father brought forth the Mother, then copulated with her and thus the Son and the Daughter were born." (Patai Chapter 5 The Kabbalistic Tetrad. Page 171)

"The Mother-Father figure as in all over the world as in the Egyptian Geb and Nut the earth and sky god and goddess, Shiva and Parvati of the Hindu myth are the components that make up the framework of the cosmogony. They are always together and never separate. This is common across mythologies worldwide."

"It is unlikely that the author of the [Kabbalistic Zohar] happened by coincidence to hit upon the same idea simply on the basis of his mystical speculations about the meaning of the first two consonants of the Tetragrammaton." (Patai Chapter 5 The Kabbalistic Tetrad. Page 172)

"In a Zoharic passage, the sexual union of the Father and the Mother...is described in graphic detail; "When the seed of the Righteous is about to be ejaculated, he does not have to seek the Female, for she abides with him, never leaves him, and is always in readiness for him. His seed flows when the Female is ready, and when they both as one desire each other, and they unite in a single embrace, and never separate. Thus the Righteous is never forsaken." (Patai Chapter 5 The Kabbalistic Tetrad. Page 172)

"It is said according to the Zohar, that "The Father loved the daughter more, while the Mother's favorite was the son. In fact, the Father's love for his daughter knew no bounds. He called her not only Daughter, but also Sister, and even Mother, and constantly kissed and fondled her. For the Mother, this was too much, she suffered pangs of jealousy and reproached the daughter, demanding that she cease beguiling her husband."

"As for the divine Mother's love for her son, she expressed it by holding him against her breast and giving suck to him and continuing to do so even after he grew up and was ready to marry."" (Patai Chapter 5 The Kabbalistic Tetrad. Page 174-176)

The son is called;

- The king
- The holy one, blessed be He
- Zoharariel (meaning splendor of Ariel)
- Ariel (a name of the altar meaning Lion of El"
- Adiryaron (the mighty one sings)

- Aktariel (my crown is El)
- Tetrasia (Four god, referring to the Tetragrammaton or to God as the ruler of the four elements air, earth, water and fire), as well as heaven seen above.

The divine daughter is called;

- Malkhuth (Kingship, the name of the tenth Sephira)
- Shekhinah (dwelling)
- Matronit (Matron or lady)
- Pearl (precious stone)
- Discarded cornerstone
- Community of Israel
- Female
- Moon
- Hart
- Earth
- Night
- Garden
- Well
- Sea
- The Supernal Woman
- The Light Woman

"According to *Joseph Gikatilla*, in the days of Abraham the Shekhinah was called Sarah, in the day so Isaac-Rebekah, and in the days of Jacob-Rachel."

"The Kabbalists not only gained insight into the mythical

nature of the Godhead from the Zoharic accounts, but also derived a quasi-sensuous emotional satisfaction from learning about the sexual and familial life of the divine tetrad which gave mythical sanction to their own life on earth." (Patai Chapter 5 The Kabbalistic Tetrad. Page 185)

"...In the Kabbalistic literature of the thirteenth century as Torah Kedumah, the primordial Torah, and is sometimes identified with God's Hokhma (Sophia), His 'wisdom,' the second emanation and manifestation of the divine power, which sprang from the hidden 'nothingness." (Scholem Chapter 2 The Meaning of the Torah. Page 41)

9

Matronit

34. The Moses-panel in the Dura Europos synagogue (3rd century A.D.), showing the Shekhina with the infant Moses in her arms.
COURTESY OF THE BOLLINGEN FOUNDATION, NEW YORK.

Shekhinah and Moses

"Here is a summary of the daughter of the Tetrad. I found the name Tetrad from this mysterious Tetragrammaton (YHWH) which is the unspeakable name of the four-person Godhead of the Kabbalah. In other words, this is the highest of the high. The divine King-daughter is known as the

Matronit, you have already been introduced to her.... as, the Shekhinah!" (Lynn Chapter 36 Come Out of Her!)

"According to Kabbalistic theory, the Matronit is but the lowest of the ten Sephirot, the mystical aspects or emanations of the Godhead, which to some extent correspond to the Gnostic aeons." (Patai Chapter 6 Matronit the Goddess of the Kabbala. Page 191)

"In the Kabbalistic Tetrad, the daughter who in addition to the old Talmudic name of Shekhinah is referred to in Jewish mystical literature as Matronita, or the Matron. Of the four persons of the Tetrad, it is s**he who plays the greatest role as the central figure** in both divine happenings and relationships which involve human fate, especially the fate of Israel. She is the central link between the ABOVE AND THE BELOW."(Patai. The Kabbalistic Tetrad. Page 161)

"The goddess thus speaks to man with four tongues;

- Keep away from me because I am a virgin
- Enjoy me because I am available to all
- Come shelter in my motherly bosom
- Die in me because I thirst for your blood

Whichever of her aspects gains momentarily the upper hand, there is a deep chord in the male psyche which power-fully responds to it. Her voices enter man and stir him, they bend man to pay homage to her, and they lure man to lose himself in her whether in love or death." (Patai Chapter 6 Matronit the Goddess of the Kabbala. Page 206)

"The Matronit, meanwhile, continued to be closely concerned with her children. Like a true goddess, she played the role of spouse as well as mother to her people. She also assumed the form of a divine queen and bride, who joined them every Friday at dusk to bring them joy and happiness on the sacred Sabbath. To this day, in every Jewish Temple or synagogue she is welcomed in the Friday evening prayers with the worlds "Come O Bride" although the old greeting has long been emptied of all mystical meaning and is regarded as a mere poetic expression of uncertain significance."

Note: does spouse and mother sound familiar, as so many of the pagan trinity myths?

If the above has you shocked, please prepare yourself for what is next. Remember, she is described as the Holy Spirit and presence of God, from what we have read, it seems as though they are saying, she is God himself, this is all from the Zohar, which is, the holiest book of the Kabbalah...

Matronit-Shekhinah Great Virgin, Mother of God

"She became the Mother of God, herself a goddess, who through ages never ceased to perform miracles and to whole direct and personal adoration is due."

"Virgin, the forces of evil could never over power the

Matronit neither Satan nor destroyer nor angel of death all whom represent forces of hell."

Note: Virgin in this realm does not mean touched by man, it means untouched by evil.

"In contrast to the pagan goddesses who all are said to have succumbed to Satan she the Shekhinah, is a cup full of blessing of which nobody has yet tasted, unimpaired, that is virginal."

Lover of men and gods
"In sharp contract Shekhinah is depicted as being enjoyed in addition to the divine King who was her lawfully wedded husband, also by Satan, other gods, heroes of Biblical history and many other men."

"A goddess behaves in accordance with her divine nature, and the human laws of sexual morality simply do not apply to her. This is common both in ancient near Eastern and Kabbalistic myths."

Yes, this says that Shekhinah lays with men...

Married to Jacob
"Zohar says Jacob became the first husband of the Matronit. However, while Jacob was alive, the union was not consummated because the polygamist that he was, he continued

to have relations with his two wives and two concubines even after the goddess attached herself to him."

"Only after his death, when his spirit entered the beyond did Jacob couple with the Matronit."

Second Husband Moses

"Having separated from his earthly wife Zipporah he was allowed to achieve what Jacob never did, to copulate with the Matronit while still in the flesh. Nothing was heard of the Matronit from the death of Moses when she took him on her wings and carried him to his unknown burial place."

Note: This is hard to read, yes, the Zohar said he (Moses) copulated with Matronit-Shekhinah in the actual flesh...

"Since Moses is said to have given up all carnal contact with his wife in order to be always ready to receive communication from the Shekhinah, it seems probable that a notion clearly stated in the Zohar was already present in rudimentary form in Talmudic times."

"The idea that the relationship between Moses and the Shekhinah was like that of HUS BAND AND WIFE. If so, there is an interesting paralleled between the Shekhinah carrying her dead husband, Moses, to his burial place, and the Ugaritic myth about Anath carrying the body of her husband-brother, Baal to his burial place."

Matronit-Shekhinah and King Solomon

"As Solomon was preparing the temple, she prepared herself for her union with her divine husband the King. She prepared a house for him in which he would take up joint residence with her, it was identical to the Jerusalem Temple. When the day arrived her Father and Mother adorned her so that her bridegroom should become desirous of her."

Explosive Origin of Matronit-Shekhinah and King Solomon

"The King and Matronit were not only brother and sister, **In fact Siamese Twins** who emerged from the womb of the Supernal mother.

"In the androgynous shape of a male and a female body attached to each other back-to-back. The King removed his sister from his back and she, after a futile attempt to reunite with him in the same position, resigned herself to the separation."

"In the heavenly realm incest does not exist according to the Zoharic text it was completely proper for the King and Matronit to marry."

"At the Divine wedding bridesmaids, groomsmen temple adorned with stones, they welcomed *him by beating their wings* with joy. After singing a song, the maidens and youths exited."

"Alone, the King and the Matronit embraced and kissed, and then he led her to the couch, and the pleasure of the King and the Matronit in each other was indescribable. She impressed her image into his body like a seal that leaves an imprint and he played betwixt her breasts and vowing in his great love that he would never forsake her."

"Some say as long as the Temple stood the King would come down from his heavenly abode every midnight. The sacred marriage thus became a daily or rather midnightly, ritual performed not by the human representatives of the god and goddess. BUT BY THE DEITIES THEMSELVES."

"This divine union had unsurpassed cosmic significance on it depended on the well-being of the whole world."

"Kabbalist (some) say they coupled once a week between Friday and Saturday and this union served as a prototype for learned men who familiar with the heavenly mysteries, couple with their wives on Friday nights in direct imitation of the union which takes place at that very time between the Supernal Couple. If the wife conceives at that hour, the earthly father and mother of the child can be sure that it will receive a soul from the ABOVE, one of those pure souls which are procreated in the divine copulation of the King and the Matronit."

"Even more when a pious earthly couple performs the act, by doing so they set in motion all the generative forces of the mythico-mystical universe. The human sexual act causes the King to emit his seminal fluid from his divine male genital and thus to fertilize the Matronit who thereupon gives births to human souls to angels."

"The Kings seminal fluid is referred to as a "river" the Shekhinah or Matronit as the "Sea" or "Living creature"

"The passage is clear; it speaks of a sexual union between the King and the Matronit and the resultant procreation by them of souls and angels." (Patai)

Defilement

"Another version says the divine copulation speaks of an annual cycle. If the people of Israel sin with tragic inevitability it enables Samael, the Satan or Azazel, to bend the Matronit to his will. Samael, in the form of a serpent, or riding a serpent, lurks at all times near the privy parts of the Matronit, in the hope of being able to penetrate her. Whether or not he succeeds in thus gratifying his desire depends on the conduct of Israel. As long as Israel remains virtuous Samael's lustful design is frustrated, but as soon as Israel sins, year after year, their sins add to Samael's power, he glues himself to the Matronit's body, with the adhesive force of resin, and defiles her."

"Once this happens, the King departs from her into the solitude of his heavenly abode. This continues until the Day of Atonement. The scapegoat, which is destined to Azazel, is hurled to its death down a cliff in the Judaea Desert. Samael, attracted by the animal offered to him, let's go of the Matronit who thereupon can ascend to heaven and reunite with her husband, the King."

"When the temple was destroyed it ended their relationship as the temple was the only place they could copulate. The Matronit was banished from her holy abode and from the Land of Israel, the King along with the Sun and Moon and all that is above and below mourned and cried with him. Both of them remained in a state of shameful nakedness. Thus the King lost stature and power and was no longer King."

"After a period of loneliness he let a slave goddess take the place of the true queen, one of the handmaidens of Matronit, Lilith. This act more than anything caused the King to lose his honor. As the Matronit her misery consisted not only in losing her husband but being banished for her palace and land. She resigned herself to being violated in exile by other gods. These unions were involuntary on her part, once other gods took possession of her, she became tied to them, and the children of these other gods, the gentiles, were able to suck from her just as the Children of Israel had done while the Temple stood."

"The Shekhinah, or Matronit, as she is now called, in her motherly love for her children, went into exile with them. This brought about a separation between her and the King, who thereupon **allowed Lilith**, queen of the demons, to attach herself to him and take the place of the Matronit as his spouse. The similarity between Matronit and Lilith is one of the rather uncanny aspects of Kabbalistic mythology." (Patai. Introduction Page 26-27)

"Whether home or exile, the Matronit is irresistibly attracted to the pious men of Israel and especially when the are engaged in either of the two most meritorious pursuits, the study the Law and the performance of good deeds. Men of such caliber make it a rule to sleep with their wives only on Friday night. Throughout the six days of the week they live as if they have been CASTRATED AND DEVOTE THEMSELVES TO THEIR HOLY WORKS."

"Whenever these men are away from their wives the SHEKHINAH COUPLES WITH THEM. Likewise, when such sages keep away from their wives because of the latter's menstrual impurity, or when they are on a voyage, SHEKHINAH JOINS THEM, NEVER ARE THEY DEPRIVED OF THE BLESSED STATE OF MALE AND FEMALE TOGETHERNESS."

Monster

"Also described as a monster. She eats the grass of a thousand mountains and devouring many beasts, drink the waters in one single gulp. Shekhinah-Matronit is described as a cosmic woman-monster with claws and arms that stretch out in 25,000 directions. In her hair are caught thousands of shields, the Moon and a comet in her tail. **From this issues Lilith** like hair and hosts of threatening war lords;

Lord of weights
Lords of severity
Lords of insolence
Lords of lords
Lords of purple

No one can escape their cruel punishment nor from Shekhinah herself.

It is consonant with this terrible aspect of the Shekhinah Matronit that also her old Talmudic role of death bringer is re-membered and revived in the Zohar which repeatedly asserts that the words of Proverbs 5:5; "Her feet go down to death," refer to Shekhinah symbolically represented by the forbidden tree which for Adam was a tree of death."

Goddess of Love and War
Her name varied from culture to culture,

- Inanna in Sumer
- Ishtar in Akkad
- Anath in Canaan
- Yet her character remained the same for centuries even millennia

Her personality exhibited everywhere the same four basic traits of charity and promiscuity, motherliness and blood-thirstiness. As Innanna she was known as a virgin "the maid Inanna", and pure Innanna. Innanna and Ishtar are used interchangeably in Babylon.

Note: Yes, the Zohar admits "she" was all of those pagan goddesses, the origin of them.

"Yet through Sumerian history she was responsible for sexual love, procreation and fertility who freely gave herself to Dumuz (Tammuz) the earliest mythical ruler of Sumer, thereafter, became the wife of ALL SUMERIAN KINGS."

"Goddess of boundless rage "the lady of battle and conflict." She armed King Hammurabi (1728-1686 B.C.)."

She had human and animal lovers

"In her human form, her love easily turned to rage, she first loved then destroyed, a long line of divine, human and ANIMAL paramours including a lion, a horse, a bird, a gardener, several shepherds, the hero Gilgamesh and Tammuz. She also was the wife of human kings such as Sargon of Agade."

"Her influence extended over all mankind and the entire animal kingdom, when she entered the Nether world, neither man or beast copulated, when she emerged, all of them were again seized by sexual desire."

"Goddess of supernatural spring, located in the region of the stars, from which flow all the rivers of the world."

"She multiplies herds and wealth, gives fertility, easy childbirth and ample milk to women, and purifies seed of men."

"She was invoked by marriageable girls and by women at the time of childbirth."

"In Armenia, she had a sanctuary at Erez in Akilisense which contained her golden statue, the daughters of noble families of Armenia used to prostitute themselves to strangers before their marriage."

"Goddess who rode on four white horses. Identified by the Greeks also with Athene and Aphrodite. Most commonly the Persian Diana or Persian Artemis. Her cult was introduced to the Persians by Artaxerxes II (404-362 BC) who built for her alters and statues in Babylon, Susa, Ekbatana, Persepolis, Baktra, Damaskos and Sardes, late Ormuzd, and the benefactor of all mankind, mother of all wisdom and queen." (Patai. Matronit The Goddess of the Kabbala. Page 186-206)

"15th-18th centuries she assumed a discrete divinity from the male deity who when contraposited to her, was referred to as her husband THE KING."

"She said to herself "It is I myself who gave birth to my

people" mother of several gods whom the fire-god was first born."

"One of her titles was sweet MISTRESS OF THE GODS."

"It was she that gave victory to her lovers, the Babylonian kings, entrusting her might armed forces to them."

"Iranian astrologists regarded her as **the personification of Venus.**"

Venus is also known as LUCIFER.

"Under the power of Venus, the rose of Lucifer was dedicated to her..."

Lucifer (Venus in the East) is glowing." (Agrippa Chapter XXVIII. What thing are under the power of Venus and are called veneral. Page 91)

Sabbath

"In the book Bahir, *Nahmanides* (*Moses ben Nahman* 1194-1270), reiterate the idea that "Remember the Sabbath day to keep it holy and Observe the Sabbath day to keep it holy," refer to two supernal sabbaths, one masculine and the other feminine. The Zohar further says it's both the mystery of the female, and the mystery of the male. The feminine Sabbath is moreover identified with Shekhinah or Sephira of

Kingship, while the male Sabbath is the Yesod (foundation_ or Tif'eret (beauty), the male aspect of the deity. In this way Shekhina becomes the bride or mate of the Sabbath-Yesod."

"In the Zohar it is said of the Mother-Father of the Tetragrammaton, "...the Male alone appears as half a body...and the female likewise, but when they join in union they seem as veritably one body...(On the Sabbath) all is found in one body, complete, for the Matronit clings to the King and they become one body, and this is why blessings are found on that day." (Patai Chapter 5 The Kabbalistic Tetrad. Page 173)

"But it is the ritual of the Sabbath, and especially of the eve of the Sabbath, that underwent the most noteworthy transformation in connection with this idea of the sacred marriage. It would be no exaggeration to call the Sabbath the day of the Kabbalah. On the Sabbath the light of the upper world bursts into the profane world in which man lives during the six days of the week. The light of the Sabbath endures into the ensuing week, growing gradually dimmer, to be relieved in the middle of the week by the rising light of the next Sabbath..."

"The Kabbalists cited three separate passages in the Talmud,..which were brought together and presented in a new light by this conception of the Sabbath as a sacred marriage. The first tells us that on the eve of the Sabbath certain rabbis used to wrap themselves in their cloaks and cry out: Come let us go to meet Queen Sabbath. Others cried: "Come, O Bride, come, O Bride." The second passage relates that on Friday evening *Simeon ben Yohai* and his son saw an old man hurrying through the dusk with two bundles of myrtle. They asked him, what are you doing with those bundles? He replied: I will honor the Sabbath with them. The third passage tells us that Torah scholars used to perform marital intercourse precisely on Friday night. These disparate reports are interpreted in the Kabbalistic books of ritual as indications that the Sabbath is indeed a marriage festival. The earthly union between man and woman, referred to in the third passage, was taken as a symbolic reference to the heavenly marriage. These themes were combined with the mystical symbolism identifying **Bride, Sabbath, and Shekhinah**. Still another mystical notion that played a part in the Kabbalistic Sabbath ritual, was the 'field of holy apple trees,' as the Shekhinah is frequently called in the Zohar. In this metaphor the 'field' is the feminine principle of the cosmos, *while the apple trees define the Shekhinah* as the expression of all the other Sefirot or holy orchards, which flow into her and exert their influence through her. During the night before the Sabbath the King is joined with the Sabbath-Bride; the holy field is fertilized, and from their sacred union the souls of the righteous are produced." (Scholem Chapter 5 Tradition and New Creation. Page 139-140)

10

Astrology

Priest gazing at the Shekhinah

Shekinah as the Moon

"The performance of the lunar Shekhinah ritual known as Kiddush Levanah is dependent on the visibility of moonlight because, according to the Kabbalah, it is by this means that the goddess is made manifest."

"In the ritual blessing for the new Moon, the Talmudists (Sanhedrin) still found an express parallel between the renewal of the Moon and Messianic redemption: 'He speaks to the Moon that it be renewed, a wondrous crown for those who were borne by me from the belly and will once cry like it grows young again and glorify their maker.' But the shift of accent to the lessening of the Moon, its changing phases, goes back to other conceptions. The Torah prescribes for the day of the new Moon a special sin offering of a he-goat-but in this prescription it is not clear for what sin the offering is made. In a Talmudic explanation we learn that God reduced the Moon, whose light was originally equal to that of the Sun. In answer to the Moon's repeated complaints, God said: "Offer up an atonement for Me, because I reduced the size of the Moon."This 'lessening of the Moon' was interpreted by the Kabbalists as a symbol of the Shekhinah's exile."

"The Shekhinah itself is the 'holy Moon,' which has fallen from its high rank, been robbed of its light and sent into cosmic exile. Since then, exactly like the Moon itself, it has shone only with reflected light." (Scholem .Page 151)

Holy Shekhinah Star

"Venus lies inside earth's orbit around the Sun and is the second in line from the Sun after mercury. Seen from the Earth Venus is by far the brightest Star in the sky after the Sun and the Moon it appears either just before dawn as the Morning Star or shortly after dust as the Evening Star. It also appears to weave a truly remarkable pattern over the time when viewed from earth. There was one astral power greater than Venus and its 40-year cycle and that was the Holy Shekhinah."

"This brilliant star would appear in the sky at periods of every 12 Venus cycles, every 480 years, and then it will shine down several times over a few years before disappearing once again. In fact the Shekhinah was and still is caused by the planets Venus and Mercury rising in conjunction, meaning that, viewed from the earth, they overlap and looked like a single, extremely bright star."

"The appearance of Shekhinah it was believed heralded the greatest moments of Israelite and Jewish history. However, particularly significant was attached to every third appearance of the Shekhinah, which took place every 1,440 years, when the brilliant object is in exactly the same place within the Zodiac, the background stars. One such appearance of the Shekhinah was due to fall at the Winter Solstice in 967 BC and Solomon ordered the land to be cleared on the hilltop to the north of the city in preparation for the laying of the foundation stone for the temple that very day. According to priestly calculations, the divine Shekhinah would appear in the dark morning sky like a brilliant beacon shortly before dawn. This date was said to be precisely 1,440 years after Noah's Ark with its surviving animals had come to rest on dry land after the great Biblical flood." (Knight and Butler. Page 8-9)

"Venus formed part of the Holy Shekhinah and it had been the sacred "hour hand" of time. It represented the supreme power of the goddess, and in fact the planet still bears her name because Venus was merely the Roman counterpart of the Egyptian Isis and Greek Aphrodite, who was herself just another version of the Great goddess.... Venus as either a male or a female representative, was viciously attacked. Lucifer, who had originally been a deity or sub-deity associated with Venues was not treated as just another name for Satan." (Knight and Butler Page 68)

"The Shekhinah was something greater than Yahweh, Astoreth or any other single god alone. Solomon understood that the light of the glorious Shekhinah heralded the mating of the total godhead with the entire world of men. The forces of the god and goddess merged as one. This was the entire world of humans linking with the realm of the gods-Earth and Heaven united as one."

"It seems that the "male" shaft of light from the star above was understood to pierce the "female" and fertile soil, as the interchange reached its climax, the identities of the male and female merged as one. As in the sexual act, they become a single entity with all attributes blurred and united. Softness and hardness, physicality and intellectuality, aggression and love, pain and ecstasy. All polarity between the female earth and the male phallus of the beam of channeled light hanged so fast they became one-male and female simultaneously, exploding in an orgasm of power and fertility."

Conclusion

Unforgivable Blasphemy

Jesus says,

> *"31 Wherefore I say unto you, All manner of sin and blasphemy shall be forgiven unto men: but the blasphemy against the Holy Ghost shall not be forgiven unto men. 32 And whosoever speaketh a word against the Son of man, it shall be forgiven him: but whosoever speaketh against the Holy Ghost, it shall not be forgiven him, neither in this world, neither in the world to come. [Matthew 12:31-32]*

"Rabbi Eliezer... objects to both the literal translation of a Biblical anthropomorphic expression and its paraphrase by the interpolation of such terms as Glory and Shekhinah. The basis of his objection to the first method is that it makes it appear as if God could directly be apprehended by human sense organs, which, of course, is untrue with reference to a spiritual deity." (Patai)

From research by *Steve Van Nattan* article *The Shekhinah Glory, the Grossest Blasphemy in all Christendom:*

"THE "SHEKHINAH GLORY" THE GROSSEST

BLASPHEMY IN ALL OF CHRISTENDOM. "But, many Fundamentalists, Charismatics, and Bible believers jabber about "the Shekhinah Glory" of God. What exquisite blasphemy. Read on, and weep for us all for letting our minds be invaded by the most pagan forms latent from ancient Babylon and Sumer." (Van Nattan)

"Apostates of the Old Testament learned from ancient Babylon and passed on to future generations through oral and written traditions to the present-day Kabbalist sects, i.e., the Lubavitch, Sephardim, Ashkenazim, etc. It is our discovery and thesis that the gnostic stream of Kabbalism, not Torah Judaism, is the real "root" of the so-called Hebrew Roots Movement." ibid

"And, in case you missed the point, Shekhinah is the wife of the Kabbalist god. When you get all prickly in a highly charged meeting and start talking about the Shekhinah glory coming down, that is THE SPIRIT OF SATAN, THE GODDESS OF PAGAN ISRAEL AND BABYLON. In your frenzied "praise and worship" services in your Charismatic church, and in all mega churches, your jumping, shouting, leaping, and acting out your emotions are NOTHING MORE THAN HAVING SPIRITUAL SEX WITH THE GODDESS, SHEKHINAH. One very well-known Christian pastor said a man came to his church during a special sermon series on Charismatic Chaos, and the man told this pastor after the service that he got an erection every time they had a praise and worship service. He fled in terror and confusion." ibid

The Kabbalah and the Talmud is the religion, the teachings and doctrine of SATAN and Christians are UNKNOWINGLY PRAISING A PAGAN SATANIC GODDESS IN THEIR SERVICE. THIS IS A CLARION CALL...

SHEKHINAH the MATRONIT aka ASTORETH, SOPHIA, ISHTAR, ISIS, DIANA, LIBERTY, SEMIRAMIS, VENUS, THE BRIGHT AND MORNING STAR, THE GREAT MOTHER GODDESS, THE DIVINE FEMININE. **LUCIFER!**

Forgive Us Father

"12 For we wrestle not against flesh and blood, but against principalities, against powers, against the rulers of the darkness of this world, against spiritual wickedness in high places." [Ephesians 6:12]

"14 For God shall bring every work into judgment, with every secret thing, whether it be good, or whether it be evil." [Ecclesiastes 12:14]

25 Jesus answered them, I told you, and ye believed not: the works that I do in my Father's name, they bear witness of me. 26 But ye believe not, because ye are not of my sheep, as I said unto you. 27 My sheep hear my voice, and I know them, and they follow me: 28 And I give unto them eternal life; and they shall never perish, neither shall any man pluck them out of my hand. ... 30 I and my Father are one. [John 10:25-30]

⁹ If we confess our sins, he is faithful and just to forgive us our sins, and to cleanse us from all unrighteousness. [I John 1:9]

The Father knows those that are HIS, would never knowingly blaspheme His Holy Spirit. If you are reading this, you now know the truth. My prayer is that all over Christendom, this name is denounced, CD's are destroyed, houses of worship are renamed, and cleansing and healing can take place. This infection was supplanted to tempt God's people to invoke a demonic spirit. Because the Father knows our heart, he has protected us for a time, know that we know the truth, WE ARE FREE.

"Now unto him that is able to keep you from falling, and to present you faultless before the presence of his glory with exceeding joy, To the only wise God our Saviour, be glory and majesty, dominion and power, both now and ever. Amen. [Jude 24-25]

In the name of Yeshua Hamashiach, Jesus the Christ.

AMEN

About the Author

V. Lynn is a published author of the *Mystery Babylon Series* of books, including *Thy Queendom Come, Lucifer Unveiled, Queen of Hell*, and *Shekhinah Glory Exposed*. Lynn is also a renowned playwright, independent journalist, researcher, and defender of the faith. V. Lynn has spent hundreds of hours of extensive on-the-ground and historical research on the Flint Water Crisis, the George Floyd riots, the Covid-19 pandemic, the United Nations, Secret Societies, and the New World Order. Ordained for missions in 2001, V. Lynn has organized ministry efforts for prisons, women's groups, youth groups, and senior citizens. V. Lynn has served as a Sunday School administrator and fine arts coach and has been active in combating childhood suicide and bullying. In philanthropic work, Lynn has spearheaded can-good, household, and infant supplies missions for communities during natural disasters. V. Lynn has dedicated her life to exposing mainstream media's destructive forces, sounding the alarm about the deceptions of the kingdom of darkness, and shining the Light of CHRIST to the world.

V. Lynn is available for writing services, coaching, publishing, and presentations. Visit www.revelationsbooks.com

BIBLIOGRAPHY

Agrippa, Henry Cornelius of Nettesheim. *Three Books of Occult Philosophy*. Ed. Donald Tyson. Vol. 11th. Woodbury: Llewellyn Publications, 2009, 1486-1535.

Babylon's Most Unholy Book-AntiChrist Talmud, Sin to Win. n.d. October 2022. <https://theserapeum.com/the-babylonian-talmud-the-jews-most-unholy-book/>.

Bension, Ariel Ph.D. *The Zohar, In Moslem and Christian Spain*. London: George Routledge and Sons Ltd., 1932.

Dan, Joseph. *Kabbalah. A Very Short Introduction*. New York: Oxford Press, 2006.

Evans, Richard. *The Kabbalah is a Hoax*. 5 September 2010. July 2022. <https://www.henrymakow.com/whats_wrong_with_the_kabbalah.html>.

Freeman, Tzvi. *The Shechinah*. n.d. October 2022. <https://www.chabad.org/library/article_cdo/aid/2438527/jewish/The-Shechina.htm>.

Gramassi, Raven. *Encyclopedia of Wiccan and Witchcraft*. St Paul: Llewelyn Publications, 2002.

Hammer, Jill. *Shekhinah*. n.d. October 2022. <https://www.telshemesh.org/shekhinah/>.

Hoffman, Michael. *Jewish Spirit Talmudist Kabbalism Discovered.* 2008.

—. *Judaism Discovered.* 2000.

Knight, Christopher and Alan Butler. *Solomon's Power Brokers. The Secrets of Freemasonry, The Church and the Illuminati.* London: Watkins Publishing, 2007.

Lilith. n.d. August 2022. <http://jewishchristianlit.com//Topics/Lilith/lilith.html>.

Lynn, V. *Thy Queendom Come; The Devils Secret Agenda.* Vol. II. Novi: Revelations Publishing House, 2022.

Mackey, M.D, Albert G. *The Symbols of Freemasonry.* New York: Clark and Maynard, 1882.

Macoy, Robert 33. *General History, Cyclopedia and Dictionary of FreeMasonry.* New York: Masonic Publishing Company, 1870.

Merriam-Webster. *Ambergis.* n.d. October 2022. <https://www.merriam-webster.com/dictionary/ambergris>.

Misler, Chuck. *Christian Video Vault.* 10 September 2022. September 2022. <https://youtu.be/Ahjx_rgRwUI>.

Mock, Leo. "Praying Towards the Shekhinah. Some Observations in Maimonide's Law of Prayeer." University of Amsterdam, 2009.

Nachtigal, Yvonne. *What is the Kabbalah and Why Is It so Bad?* 9 May 2018. July 2022. <https://christianobserver.net/what-is-the-kabbalah-and-why-is-it-so-bad/>.

Patai, Raphael. *The Hebrew Goddess.* Ktav Publishing House Inc., 1967.

Philo. n.d. October 2022. <https://en.wikipedia.org/wiki/Philo>.

Scholem, Gershom. *On the Mystical Shape of the Godhead; Basic concepts in Kabbalah*. Ed. Joachim (translater) Neugroschel. New York: Schoken Books, 1991.

The Serapeum. *The Babylonion Talmud the... most Unholy Book*. n.d. October 2022. <https://theserapeum.com/the-babylonian-talmud-the-jews-most-unholy-book/>.

—. *The Kabbalah and It's Symbolism*. Ed. Ralph (translater) Manheim. New York: Schocken Books, 1965, 1969.

Urbach, Ephraim E. *The Sages; Their Concepts and Beliefs*. Ed. Israel Abrahams and Translator. Vol. II. Jerusalem: Magnes Press; The Hebrew University Jerusalem, 1987.

Van Nattan, Steve (Editor). *The Shekhinah Glory, the Grossest Blasphemy in all Christendom*. n.d. August 2022. <http://www.blessedquietness.com/journal/housechu/shakhina.htm>.

QUEEN

OF HEAVEN ~~X~~ HELL

THE DIVINE FEMININE DECEPTIO|